# Midwinter Transport

# Midwinter Transport

Anne Bromley

Carnegie-Mellon University Press
Pittsburgh 1985

# ACKNOWLEDGMENTS

The author expresses gratitude to the editors of the following magazines in which many of the poems in this collection first appeared: *Another Chicago Magazine:* "Mission Bay"; *Calyx:* "Anniversary in Your Absence," "For Christine"; *En Passant:* "Ending a Climb"; *Kayak:* "Banks Close Too Early for Painters," "Cat in the Shell, Moon on the Wane," "Intersection at the Zero Hour," "1:00 A.M. Memorial Day," *and* "Sleepwalking"; *Loon:* "Miniature"; *Massachusetts Review:* "Slow Men Working in Trees"; *Mississippi Valley Review:* "Breaking Bones," "Briefly Visible," *and* "Night Running"; *Panache:* "Dog Day," *and* "Something in this Room Reminds You of a Time"; *Partisan Review:* "Birds in the Hand"; *Poet and Critic:* "Teel St. Trailer Court," *and* "The New Lunch Poems"; *Prairie Schooner:* "Misreadings at a Desk Near a Window"; *Rhino:* "One Shell Lies in the Alcove," *and* "Taming the Matador"; *Small Moon:* "Ritual"; *Spoon River Quarterly:* "Before America," "Focus," "I am Watching You," *and* "My Mother's Face Never Moved"; *Willmore City:* "Election Day, 1976"; *Tucson Poetry Quarterly:* "To Those Who Do Not Remember Their Dreams".

The publication of this book is supported by grants from the National Endowment for the Arts in Washington, D.C., a Federal agency, and by the Pennsylvania Council on the Arts.

Carnegie-Mellon University Press books are distributed by Harper & Row.

Library of Congress Catalog Card Number   85-70429
ISBN 0-88748-016-0
ISBN 0-88748-017-9 (pbk.)
Printed and bound in the United States of America
First Edition

# CONTENTS

## I. Night Running

My Mother's Face Never Moved / 11
Ritual / 12
Dusting His Mahogany Desk / 13
Something in This Room Reminds You of a Time / 14
Breaking Bones / 15
To Those Who Do Not Remember Their Dreams / 16
Midwinter Transport / 17
Misreadings at a Desk Near a Window / 18
A Second of Silence / 20
Night Running / 21
Election Day, 1976 / 22
1:00 AM Memorial Day / 23

## II. Through the Ravine

April Afternnon / 27
Briefly Visible / 28
Folds of White / 29
On the Crest of I Love You / 30
Collecting Stones for a Game of *Go* / 31
Cross Country / 32
Ending a Climb (For John) / 33
Miniatures / 34
The Bandaid Leaks Blood / 35
Anniversary in Your Absence / 36
Teel St. Trailer Court / 37
I Am Watching You / 38
Focus / 39
Mission Bay / 40

## III. Frayed Angels

Seen from Mt. Sugarloaf — Prose for Austin Church / 43
For Austin Church (1820-1876) / 44
Slow Men Working in Trees / 45
The New Lunch Poems / 46
Dog Day / 51
For Christine / 52
One Shell Lies in an Alcove / 53
My Father at 60 / 54
My Guests / 55
Frayed Angels / 56
Outside the Hotel Coronado / 59
No Saving Grace / 60
Taming the Matador / 61
Before America / 62
Notes on a Recital / 64
Every Scene We Walk into is Open-Ended / 65
Birds in the Hand / 66

## IV. Voice in the Bowl

Traveling Music / 69
Rilke's Daydream / 70
White Cat in the Shell, Moon On the Wane / 71
Dwarf in the Rock / 72
Sleepwalking / 73
The Doodler / 75
Banks Close Too Early For Painters / 76
Intersection at the Zero Hour / 77
Voice in the Bowl / 78
The Planet Is Too Cold For Invaders / 79
Waiting For Instruction / 80

*We keep remembering something different from what we celebrate, to commemorate a glimpse that we have forgotten, as a stone slab may commemorate a resurrection. There were golden wagons moving without wheels over the desert in a little cloud, with four tall torches lighting the way in the mind of one who saw and tried to tell us. And we listened and made wheels.*

*— W.S. Merwin, from* Houses and Travelers

# I.

# Night Running

# My Mother's Face Never Moved

throughout the funeral ... even as her nails
dug into my skin when the elegy was said
she wore no black
or gray ... reminding me that Lou Burgess hated
black on women
unless the neckline plunged or the back was open
my mother wore green, pine green
and her hair was coiffed in a way I remember
a long time ago in a photograph
with Lou
with my father
with Lou's wife ...
Lou's son and I were playing with trains
in the basement ... a party upstairs
the tinkle of glass, Lou's deep laugh
my mother winking at him from across the room
I went up for Cokes
and saw Lou's hand on my mother's waist
in the crowded kitchen ... he filled the empty glasses
then sent me off
back down to the basement
I got tired of watching those wormy trains
the planned breakdowns
the fake collisions
the rubber tunnel in the rubber mountain
and the stupid toy soldiers trying to sabotage
the same old tracks ... I kept listening
for whole sentences upstairs, some clue
to the dirty words that fell like tinsel
on a naked pine

## Ritual

Today I walked the beach where we were married
needing some form of re-enactment. It was 5 a.m.
on a dim August morning—too early for anything
to be moving. We were like a secret clan that gathers
in darkness in remote places, hurrying to get through
its ritual before dawn.

We had carefully chosen the words to be spoken
yet they were barely audible above the waves.
Our parents' eyes were tired. It was too early for them.
Looking past us they did not seem to mind
that God was not mentioned.

My bare feet fill holes of sand with more sand
in the spot where your grandmother stood. She had been
                                                    unsteady,
unsure of this, up all night praying for us, trying to create
an appropriate temple.
She walked to the shore and saw her dead husband
in a trick of mist. Somewhere
in the middle of your part, she became weak.
Her legs gave way and there was no going on when she fell.
No need for rings, a pronouncement, a final kiss.

We turned away from the ocean
realizing how short some rituals can be,
following her as she rode in the handswing of my father
and your brother. She led us
across the cold morning sand.

## Dusting His Mahogany Desk

I follow the grain as if it were a map.
The drawers empty his diary, his sketches of a bridge,
the obsolete slide-rule
and the ruby he kept in the inkwell for good luck.
I spin the globe he always left on a side table, always
turned to India where he wanted to build a highway.
I see him resting his head on the blotter at midnight.
A pencil drops and one suspender falls to his waist.
I imagine him dreaming.

A bay mare whinnies from the wallpaper as she gallops
across a flat field over jonquils. Sweat running down her neck
vaporizes the old glue. Ends of yellow paper curl
near his wrist. Tiny yellow clusters fall out of the wall,
litter the floor where his ankles cross.
He had always confused them with daffodils. The small, rush-like
leaves fall around his collar, tickling his neck.
The mare snorts their fragrance, her head nuzzling
the petalled lips. His arms hug the desk.
His eyelids move and she trots around the room,
her mane flying out like long grass.

## Something in This Room Reminds You of a Time

when a woman left her skirt on a chair.
Other articles of clothing left a trail to another room,
not the bedroom.

A trenchcoat on the sofa's arm reminds you of how hard
the rain came down that night, like arrows
speeding into the desert. Your wet hands
hailed the Yellow Cab while marquee lights rainbowed
in the blur of rain.

After the torrent she left in the morning.
You remember the stir of loneliness,
how she stood in the doorway
swinging the door between her palms.
You remember her laughing at your polka-dotted shorts
and think how lucky
to be saved by good riddance.

You gather strands of red hair left on the rug,
tuck them into a white envelope
and carefully print her name on the outside.

## Breaking Bones

she comes swimming
into your eyes
those eyes that follow her follow
the length of her leg like knives
her manikin sway in a room full of dancers ... the display
window blasted away and you are wanting
to cry in the desert of her neck

well-worn, you continue to compete
wanting to make her fly like unraveled chicken wire
against the wall of night ... break her back
let her know
she will never know
a man like you, the only straw in an empty barn

chicken bones gather dust on a crumb-filled plate
... the flesh eaten
like the idea of loving her, how it decays
... stranger bones laid bare
you beg for the slap of her wet hair
waxen in the thankless moonlight

the sun, luminous pearl
foundering in muscled clouds ... there is
that imprint on her face as if
she had slept on corduroy .. a patch of ruin
across one eye and you will not take this
any longer ... the rash of sparrows
against the sky

## To Those Who Do Not Remember Their Dreams

No matter
The fog of not knowing
Will disperse at dawn and yet
There is that clawing
Desire to recall
The night's occupation, the visits
To the Empire State Building from where
Your bed spun like a button on a needle
And you watched
Clinging to the bedposts
As the city lights went out like stars
Or the return to a room of all those people
You have been preparing speeches for
And there you are
With oatmeal in your mouth
Or the desperate running through a desert
Chased by a faceless man in a helicopter
With no sage large enough to hide you
Or the last morning you spent with your mother
The blood pooling from her mouth
The cup of your father's hand

## Midwinter Transport

My right hand in your left pocket
we wade through the deep slush . . . uneasy passage
through this bitch
of freezing rain and a million pins prick our faces
getting at the new skin
our love has taken on

There are rhythms, midwinter
dancing in our blood . . . large bowls
of hot soup on the table
a loaf of bread already torn apart
and the temperature will drop tonight
dogs will glide over smooth puddles
with the moon glaring at them like a face left in the street
. . . crystal casts on the oak limbs
we are under a glass globe careening
toward a warmer planet
. . . the spell of chimney smoke before we break

# Misreadings at a Desk Near a Window

## I

You have been reading a play that baffles you
and a calico cat outside your window is tied
to a yellow string
connected to the wrist of a woman in a pink bathing suit
watching a soap opera next to a man snoring.
The cat rubs his neck against the bush and eats its leaves.
You watch the string tug at the woman's wrist.
She spills a glass.
You turn the page.

## II

Your stained-glass owl twirls on the curtain rod
as motes of sunlight come dancing through his purple eyes.
His head is turned to the rocks on the sill,
reminders of rivers you have waded in. *As the World Turns*
is interrupted by a commercial.
The man wakes up.

## III

Your telephone bill stares up at you
through the glass paperweight.
The digits of a call to Phoenix are magnified
and you hear the voice you pleaded with for hours.
The pepperomia yields northward in its pot
near a porcelain frog covering an ink stain.
The cat eating the bush has become tangled
in the yellow string.

IV

Your pens are held in the holes of a small globe
that needs dusting, a sixteenth century version of the world
with a smiling dragon that scuttles along
the Tropic of Cancer.
You begin to understand what has happened—
Vladimir says, "Oh pardon! I could have sworn it was a carrot!"
in response to Estragon who thought it was a turnip.
You have discovered that they are hungry.
They have to make it last, whatever it is.

## A Second of Silence

Then much noise.
The actor dies knowing he will come back
in a different hat.
No applause, only silence and second-hand clothes.
The fact of it
has nothing to do with seeing it happen.
It is not gasps and blood and
falling about. It's just a man failing to reappear.
Now you see him, now you don't ... an endless time
of never coming back. It is the gap
the actor cannot see, and when the wind blows through it,
it makes no sound.

There must have been a moment, at the beginning
when he could have said no
but somehow he missed it.

## Night Running

Wind disturbs the net of stars lighting the distance
to your house. It is surrounded
by emphatic pines, reminders to the dark
that it is only light that cannot be reached.
I hear your words, crystals glistening in the receiver
winding like breath through my bones . . . I move on
to where you are waiting.

A window passes
holding lavendar light, someone's decision
not to sit in the dark.
I watch the white balloon caught in a telephone wire.
It sways above the trees, advertising its loss.

I bend into the last hill
breaking patches of ice, my face yielding
to the snow's invitation to sleep . . . I fall
and blood leaks along a crevice in my palm.
Birch limbs are a tapestry of nerves
above this uncertain surface. How much farther
to that house where your face comes and goes at the window?

## Election Day, 1976

You are walking out of town far from the streetlights.
You forgot how short the days are becoming. In the moon's
half-light a hill rises as bare tree limbs claw at the stars.
Somewhere back in town votes are being counted in well-lit
rooms. You had not counted on going this far as the cold
gathers at your neck. You hear a woman's voice calling from
a screen door that dinner is ready. She makes you hungry,
and cows you cannot see lay down in the dark field to eat or
dream of eating. There seems to be a light ahead, out of place
on this empty road. On both sides of you are cornfields, stalks
waving like ghosts. You try to remember the farmer's name who
sold this land a century ago, who settled his affairs, cast his
vote and went to sea, never having seen it before. The road
is becoming a wave and you are way past any farmhouse now.
The light you thought you saw is only a sign saying: "You
are leaving . . ." You can't make out the name.

# 1:00 AM Memorial Day

Two white crows swim in the heavy rain, dodging
hailstones. The wind splits open their wings
like envelopes.

You are healing from the assault,
surprise invasion in the early hours.
A man boring a flashlight into your eyes
says, "Open them, bitch!"
No dream was ever like this.
Your lover's split forehead,
popped screen on the lawn. He was a stranger with an eye
for open windows, sleeping women, weaponless men.
He is everyone's fear.

Yet his eyes were the color of terror, the whites
stretched so far the pupils could pop their sockets.
You got to the phone — "Operator, get me the . . ."
No answer. You fake it.
"You bitch, I'm gonna cut you too!" But mercy has him
at the door on the next dial tone.
The flashing red lights, the four-inch knife
he never used. Bloody flashlight, your naked lover
holding his head. You have seen everything
and it is over . . . and over

in small talk over coffee
in drugstores
in bookstores
in department stores

the featureless manikins sway when you brush by
you feel them reach for you
sixty seconds played back, played back
each time without warning.

The two white crows cannot fly in the heavy rain.
The peonies droop, their petals spread over the yard
like bits of pink tissue.
The man is running down
every alley he can find,
"I'm gonna cut you you you" he breathes
knifeless.

# II.

# Through the Ravine

## April Afternoon

anchored in a groundswell beneath shadeless trees
we lie on our stomachs
watching spindly-legged kids swarm out of a schoolbus.
Their bookbags spill yellow sheets
filled with long division while Superman and Wonder Woman
vie for the same space in deep pockets,
their balloon voices mumbling between notebooks.

I pull gum wrappers from your pocket, Doublemint
green and Spearmint white neatly folded
like notes to yourself, things to remember
to do tomorrow. They drift

into the shadow of a plane flying low
that waves a pale ad against the sky—a place to eat
or a brand of tire that assumes we will look up.
Our afternoon

retreats into windows with the hiss
of two bicycles, their chrome glistening
an asphalt hill. So steep a grade

leaves them breathless at the top.
We watch the man lean over
and feel the warm air he blows
into the shell of the woman's ear.

## Briefly Visible

This day is as memorable
as dinners I had as a child
always preceded by the grace I memorized
like faint light in the alley
and the deep-voiced bell in the church
tolling the hour of five.
"What is that on the roof?" you ask
accidentally pouring wine into the plants.

"Only rain." It graces us as if
it had come out of hiding. You open the door
and wave at the hills . . . the backs of heads
with wet hair.

The evening is memory. It explains the log in the fire
becoming a guitar . . . no
it is the neck of that guitar and Segovia rising
out of the chimney, or
a bald man hunched over a wooden box
in a straightback chair. His fingers are only briefly visible
as they waver along the frets
meeting the rain that quiets
the steam rising out of manholes.

## Folds of White

This woman can only stare at the bloodstained sheets
This man can only sit on a rock facing an island
He wants to touch with his whole hand
While the gull dutifully scours the beach
Soaring on to other desertions

What's left is the woman waving the fog from her eyes
Asking where is he?
And this man remembering or trying to remember
The day he first saw black, yellow, the shape of fruit
The skin breaking in his mouth

This woman wraps the sheet around her waist
Walks to the door saying that to know the name
Is not to know everything
What's left is to ask the sandpiper
If a man wearing a blue shirt happened by

## On the Crest of 'I Love You'

your island will disappear
and in its place
will sit a pot-bellied fisherman
playing a flute to a bitten moon
soon to be as full as he

you have said it means to give all
and yet what finally comes is an exchange of shells
for wine . . . that same fisherman waving his net
to the drunken sailor squatting on a reef
another sea away
while applauding fish leave their nests

you, like them, are past fear now
on the shore of your watching
this island pulled along, scraping the sky's edge
like a kite let go

it drapes the beak of a gull
and you watch the wind turn over the starfish
its pink belly glistens
in the dark and promising sand

## Collecting Stones For a Game of *Go*

A fish is tossed from the surf
A rabbit lies dead in the sand
pooling his blood in the shell's mouth
The ignorant wind
riffles the wings of a swallow trapped in chapparal
I collect small stones for a game of *Go*

Found in tidepools
there are no white ones . . . only black and gray
Enough for one player . . . they are the perfect size
for the wooden board set on a flat rock in the garden
The game must wait for the white stones
while every day a line of children runs into the sea
breaking like beads

## Cross Country

You reach behind the flexible structure for the lines
and laugh, noticing how curiously
one is welded to the other—

*the act of running* plus
*the tentative cheer for the sunset in the park*

so easily. Try to believe
in the way a runner is like a tentative cheer
and listen to your feet

touching the crab grass
squeaking from the rain you ignored
as if to be soaked
is to be soaked free,

or throw them out and begin again with others.
It will creep back.
The tentative cheer came before you thought of it:
a given
in your systems approach to the world. You notice
the indivisibility
of your leg to your foot to the clover to the horizon
behind the voyeur's binoculars. You are a figure
fixed in the centerfold of his consciousness—
*Woman running*

and you reach for the line
as you reach for the pulse in your neck
as if it were a petulant fly throbbing under cellophane.

Sweat beads at your forehead
and you run another mile, unfolding your fists
letting the air sift through your fingers.

## Ending a Climb (For John)

You feel the hollow of your helmet
and scoop the sweat out
as you sit in that rope-swing hung from a point
in the sky. All you care about now
before caring later in the womb of your bedroom,
making climbing motions in your sleep
is drying out
measuring the distance between yourself
and the next peak
like a woman stringing a clothesline
between tenements.

You hang there not believing you bled so much
on those rocks
and you want to go back to scour the crevices
clean, cover up your mess, pull up the ropes
throw down the bolts and petons that laddered you
to this end.
You want to scream nonsense
about being a god who swings into sunset
across purple mountains, camel-backs
lying motionless—too tired and too old
to care about moving you
as you are moved.

## Miniature

It is not often that we just sit like this.
We are always off in the mornings, pushing in
the stem of the alarm
to go about our busyness in front of mirrors
or pouring cereal, finding right keys
for cars and desk drawers. We are
up to our necks in paper.

Once in a while the phone rings when I least expect it.
It is you shoving papers aside, careening the paperwight
I gave you. Inside it
snow is shaken onto watery fixtures — a house
that remains still even as you shake it
and the figure of a man walking
in the snow, carring logs,
his face stinging and groping for a clearness.
He enters a door opening to fire
and a woman also waiting for the sky to clear
and settle upright on paper.

## The Bandaid Leaks Blood

You ask where is that place
you can't touch ... I say nowhere
The wind makes every pore ooze pain
Uncoils the white snake of memory —
Old wound that won't quit
Yet the mountain insists

on being seen ... black wart on the horizon
It expects no comfort for what it is
The hidden streams bleed snow
down its far side
The scars will show in the scorch of summer
Red water in the sink gurgles down the drain
You close your eyes
pressing your lips into my palm as if
fitting your face into a mask

## Anniversary in Your Absence

A thousand miles away I trace
with cold fingers a picture of you and your brother
under a magnolia tree. This is
the first year I have had nothing
of yours to touch and I am burning
bagels in the broiler. The sound
of that sentence is the happiest part of the day.

Today you are the imagined face
of a camera. What would you be
if I had run out of film?

A dream usurps your presence in the picture.
I answer the knock at the door

out of context, leaning over in sleep
to feel your face. It is never enough
to be held in
by a damp nightgown in the hollow
of a bed, of a tree
where only your brother stands
and my knees are coming
to my face.

It is a strange and permanent postition
of longing.

# Teel St. Trailer Court

Marigolds in a white box. No love
has yet been made. Only white cattle
floating through the tall grass.
Their eyes, heavily lidded, blink at the sun
melting first light on the soft curve of road.

There are men and women living in trailers.
Their lights are tiny suns rising above checkered curtains.
There is no time for making love.
Their shadows move about the small rooms,
        packing bag lunches, drinking instant coffee,
their fingers tapping on formica counters.

He will drop her off at Hubbell Lighting,
driving on to Corning Glassworks.
He will pick her up at four, drive on
to Little People Day Care where
their son has been fingerpainting blue suns and purple grass.

Son and mother mow the lawn. His short legs and toy mower
echo her longer stride.
His tennis shoes dry on the porch. His tee-shirts
blow urgently on the clothesline.

His father puzzles under the hood of a red MG;
he believes there is no reason why
he cannot get it back on the road. Golden rod
surrounds the cinderblocks, and the lights go out
at ten o'clock. No love has yet been made
as the cornflowers bloom before dawn.

## I Am Watching You

watch me as I lean on the arm of your husband
I am drawn into that white water of your eyes—
the whirlpool of doubt

I ask you to believe that I have known
what you know
cups twirling on their sides
then teetering on the edge of the table
where you shared meals with him
corner-conversations at the kitchen table
where the fruit ripened in baskets
Too long it went uneaten

Not long ago
I created that gesture
saying I would take what was required
not willing to let suffice
the shirt on my back
I grasped for the sequined gown
I knew its fierce glitter on my breast
would blind him
Nothing could stop me then

Today I hold your stone glare
that baleful way you dig into the pockets
of your jacket, pulling away the tight threads
You want to rip open the insides of warmth
to let in the cold
Your eyes direct pins to my neck
as if I were that doll sitting on your dresser
The one he gave you
won at a carnival last year

## Focus

A child plays with my binoculars. She tires at looking
down on the same river. She has counted every rooftop
and knows the mountain range by heart. Now she is bored
and turns to marvel at the blue in my eyes, the cracks
in my lips. She says she sees me better with her big eyes,
that it is fun to watch my face. I make a face at her
and think about your car moving toylike
through diminishing hills. You can't imagine
how small you are becoming.

## Mission Bay

Children run into the water that invites them.
A man tells a woman that the wedding is off.
There are red markers to indicate "No Swimming."

Tri-colored sails glide over the mirror of bay.
A tri-colored jersey zooms by.
The conversation is over but for — "You'd have worn
blue cords, anyway, you bastard," and the beercan
in her hand settles like the sea at sunset, flattening
in the stillness of her clenched palm.
He twirls the tab around a pencil
like a child discovering a new toy.

A sail has tipped over
but the sailor is not chagrined.
She shrieks with delight that she has lost control
and the water is roaring.

There are no palms on Fiesta Island, the distance
runner's dream of solitude before the fog lifts.
Two flags at half-mast above the San Diego Hilton.
Who has died?
The world could exist on Mission Bay

where sailors and runners
have stopped reading newspapers forever.
Yet there is nothing cryptic here. Mission Bay
cannot lie about its bald love of sand and palms.

It proclaims no metaphor,
no dark vision of undertow

just flickering shadows of boys
setting fire to an old man's tent.

# III.

## Frayed Angels

.

## Seen From Mt. Sugarloaf—Prose For Austin Church

From this tower the Connecticut Valley is a patchwork. A
toy tractor churns red dust. Through the binoculars I see a
farmer with red hair and freckles. He spits on the dirt as
the river bends every semblance of line. A child runs up the
spiral stairs of the look-out tower, yells down to his parents,
"Look at me!" The farmer spits again.

Something happened down there very suddenly one hun-
dred years ago. Austin Church of South Amherst died on
the 12th. It was said that he had been cutting corn at 4
p.m. a short distance from his house. He did not come
home at the usual time, but no one worried until 8 p.m. A
search was made and he was found lying in a cornfield
nearly dead. He had dug graves all summer. He had red
hair. He tired easily after a day of digging graves. Spitting
on the dirt, "What the hell, it's all the same. Heavy
corpses." And picking corn: "An ear here, an ear there.
Everywhere an ear." Austin Church laughed at himself and
had no thought of dying on the 12th. Heat exhaustion. He
had scanned the horizon a dozen times that day praying for
sunset. The last grave had been like digging straight to
China. For the mayor. "May he rest in peace. Good man,
Mayor Childress. But heavy. Must've weighed at least 300
pounds." Mayor Childress almost broke Austin Church's
back. He left Austin Church too tired for farming that day.
"Diggin' and farmin'—one's the same as the other."

From this tower I can't make out that the grass is going to
seed, that the flickers are getting restless to migrate. There
are no autumnal facts to be insisted on. Just echoes of a
man who talks to himself down below and everywhere an
ear.

## For Austin Church (1820-1876)

What kills is something autumn
when everything is a matter of color
and the fire and summer vines cross
in your woodland. Morning deer keep coming
to sip from your spring, their backs
shuddering in the light.

A bear prowls near your barn and I remember the end.
We came to watch you die with offerings of wine
and suggestions that you live out the last days
in the South. What you left behind was a sound
that hangs where I stand now, a trespasser —
"Let in the bear."

## Slow Men Working in Trees

You saw a sign once: SLOW — MEN WORKING IN TREES
and you thought it was perfect
for slow men to be working in trees, that a tree
is the only place where a slow man can work
without fear of being rushed
into completing what a quick man puts before him.

You are an engineer and measure the slowness
of men working against your highways, your bridges.
They never see the heart
of your plans. They hesitate and you want to break
their slanted drawing boards.

It comes as no surprise to you that they have left
the drawing room for trees, that they work slowly
into the night while you try to sleep
next to a woman with no patience for slow men.
Drawing the curtain doesn't help. You hear the branches
tapping on the pane.

They must know that this is the hour least easy to bear
as you ask what right
slow men have to be working in your tree.
You decide it must come down and repeat this aloud
to the woman next to you. You hear yourself screaming
above the scratches on the window
that tomorrow the slow men will be gone
and you will be left alone with their sign.

# The New Lunch Poems

Woman Beside Fountain

A woman sits on a stone bench beside an abstract fountain. The water is turned off. She sits with her checkered slacks rolled up to her knees trying to get some sun. She opens a yellow plastic container holding her lunch—a green salad topped with Thousand Island dressing. The salad is accompanied by a Weight-Watchers lemon-lime soda. She sits on a light red jacket that shows her nameplate hanging over the edge of the bench—Millie Green. The sun clashes with the haze through the empty fountain. The woman peels a banana, uncrosses her legs. There is mixed fruit in another plastic container. It is clear, and each piece of apple, orange, and pear is partially visible. The woman squints, then eats faster, moving over into the shade of the fountain's arc. When she has finished eating, she stretches out on the bench, dreaming she is a great stone lioness guarding a temple.

## Man Beside Tree Trunk

A man scratches a design in a tree trunk. He is waiting for his picnic companion. She is late, and he carves the complete floorplan of his childhood house in Red Oak, Iowa. He is not hungry for the food she has packed. He remembers the beer his grandfather made in the bathtub, his grandmother fainting when she heard that Rudolph Valentino died. The woman's hand touches his shoulder as he carves the last corridor. He dreams he is a Medieval miniaturist whose beetles advance slowly under deep fibers of vegetation.

Today's Special

He walks up to the gray-haired lady behind the yellow
counter and orders the usual—medium hamburger, fries,
and a Coke. And, oh, make that with tomatoes and mayo.
Hold the lettuce. She stands there in her nurse-white
uniform holding a head of lettuce like a bouquet. He
thinks of the layers that lead to nothing, then yells for a
milkshake, extra thick. The white bubbles in the meat pop.
He reaches into his pocket for change and watches the
crowded grill—patties, bacon, eggs, toast, home fries, all in
some great mural called Today's Special. The fan blows his
napkin into a woman's face. She is about to bite into tuna
and lettuce on wheat toast. The register rings up the totals
as he slips into a booth. He closes his eyes at the first bite
of food—his first, maybe last meal of the day.

# Rain

A bag lady stands outside the Trailways station eating a popsicle. She hears the transistor radio warning, huddles closer to the Billy Joel poster int the corner. Her argyle socks rumple at her ankles. She wipes the sweat from her neck with a pink Kleenex, looks up at the sky wishing and fearing it will come. "90% humidity," she mutters, "It might as well." And then it comes . . . as if from out of hiding. Her paperbag tips over, and balls of yarn roll into a gutter.

## Graveyard Respite

A woman walks to the cemetery
with a brown bag of lunch —
tuna salad, chips, and two carrots.
A Pepsi in her other hand.

This is the tenth straight day
of ninety degrees and ninety percent humidity.
She looks for a tree
as if looking for a lost relative.

Leaning against the headstone
of Josiah Whitemiller: b. 1816 d. 1878
she eats her lunch
and will carry his markings back to work.

# Dog Day

I place my hand on your neck wound
from last night — bloodstiffened
fur like red stalks growing
and I need to know
why you do not feel my hand, my hand
so curious that it touches and remains
on the open wound, a meeting place
of teeth and flesh that invites me to consider
how it was for you
how you left him when it was over
with his red teeth

you took yourself to a park
where you thought it was snowing
There in dog pain under a crescent moon
you rolled and rolled on white ground
craving snow
to fill the deep red hole

## For Christine

You left me. I can forgive that.
What I cannot forgive is being too young
to know you. There is only a picture of you
before you married Dad and a memory
of a walk along the beach.
Holding my hand as if it were the last hand to hold,
you stopped suddenly and fell at my feet. I pressed
myself upon you like someone pressing on a bruise.
Blood on your mouth—
A stranger stopped to ask my name, where I lived.
Holding your hair I could not tell him. His eyes
scanned the empty beach. Only sand, gulls
and you, Christine. He did what was left
and I cannot forgive the blood
on his white shorts as he ran with you
in his arms to where I could not follow.
You knew all along
I'd never be able to keep up.

## One Shell Lies In The Alcove

There is a shadow in the shell —
the palpable absence of some creature
A woman is dying in damp sheets
She is hungry
and a nurse searches her arm
for the last available vein ... I hold
her bruised hand and watch peaks on a graph
turn to waves
She moans something about lifting a bottle
from the sea, the teasing message on yellowing paper
scrawled in another language

She died in autumn
when trees toss their leaves like hats
She stirred only once in her sleep
as if shaken by the voice of an old lover
or an idea that came to her

like a red balloon crossing the river
swept by wind
the pressure of what is unseen

## My Father At 60

In only his shorts he lies in the wide yard
getting brown. He rubs an apple between his palms
closing his eyes to let his teeth break the cold
red skin ... he tastes the snow in his mouth

He looks at the trim shrubs, at the dog
peeing on his blue spruce ... at the day
giving way and further on
the soft green mounds he made with his rake
all afternoon. He feels the wind
of my child running to a still pile
feels the grass sticking to his face
like moss on a smooth stone

## My Guests

They are asleep in my bedroom
Father's rings on the dresser
Mother's make-up on the desk
My towels drape their suitcase
I have been occupied
I tend to them ... placing water
on the bedstand, a blanket at their feet
He crosses her hip with his leg
She makes a low noise I've heard before in their house
They will leave in the morning but not before
Removing those voluptuous sheets

# Frayed Angels

## I. Bag Lady

An old woman wears a cardigan sweater
put on backwards
She limps past the turnstiles
past the busses she never rides ... in her pocket
is a ball of threads collected from the coats
of strangers two steps above her
on the escalators

She walks through the station repeating
"I spit blood."
She stops to stare at herself in a gum machine mirror
Parts her hair in the middle
then combs it with her fingers down her brow
like a child in a daguerrotype
Her clear eyes, pale blue of cornflowers


## II. The Subway Prophet Said

he wished it were true now as then
when the moon was so close she was on top of us
all the time —
bright as day, she could have crushed us
and when she was new
she was like a black umbrella rolling around in the sky
When she was waxing she came at us
with horns so low
they could puncture mountains

he told me he had found my soul—
plastic globe in a toy store
said when he threw it high in the air
it changed shapes, became pearlike
the way the earth really is

When I last saw him
he carried a tall black ladder and a compass
He walked north
then south
Said he wanted to climb onto the moon
the next time her face was full


III. She Was the Bad Girl

who set her dolls on fire
one August afternoon
She got tired of playing maid to them
changing their clothes ten times a day—
a dress, a blouse for every mood in every doll—
pulling the tangles from their hair
uncrossing their legs

She lined them naked in a row
facing the sky
so she could see their frozen blue eyes
She stared long and hard at Chatty Cathy—
the string that made her talk
curling into a cinder

She sat cross-legged on the hot side-walk
wanting an end to dolls
but wanting their eyes to remain
Ice storms in plastic
promising a village buried in snow
and everything sleeping on soft pillows

## IV. Wanting the Wild Man

First day you were a stranger
bare to the sky
Head and heart scratching around in your tongue
That's a cozy niche, wild man

You mistake me for something else
the way you talk on and on
like I was one of your ears

Mud under your arms, mud sliding
down the sides of your boots
You've got that thick, stormy kind of hair
and dirty nails ... you look like
you've always had a button missing

Clouds glow when I go home
A rich warm rose sails out til dark
I want to eat and go to bed early
Get down and wait for the dead light
to come crawling through my window
watch the fake snow settle in the paperweight
and dig into my pillow, wild man
try to find out your secret

## Outside The Hotel Coronado

The old man sits on the veranda watching his young wife
take a picture of a surfer. She turns and calls to him but
all he can do is read her lips. The battery in his hearing
aid has gone dead. She wants to change her clothes and go
swimming. That means he must sit there even longer in the
sun. She wants him to join her in the water, says it will be
good for him, will relax him. But he does not want to leave
the hot bench. There are puddles near his feet where
negligent bathers have dripped. He mutters that there is
nothing dry left. He hates the humidity, how it gets into his
bones, how he feels the wet even before it touches him. He
misses Arizona and goes to sit in the car parked in the sun.
He rolls up the windows, locks the door. He stares long into
the chrome bumper of the car parked in front of him.

## No Saving Grace

You have told her
No Secrets
and empty your drawers of all the letters
you wanted to burn but saved
in case This One left you ... she looks at you
as if she were trying to identify a plant
and you feel your name stretching out
into something unpronounceable
when the drawer falls to your foot
and you swear your foot has left you
when you are left only
with the afterspasm of insult
the mustache painted on your face

# Taming the Matador

They release you into the ring
Let you stand in your own shadow
waving a gaudy cape

You cannot hear the bull behind your back
The soundtrack has gone dead
Someone hurls an orange at the screen

What you fear is slow motion
The eyes of the bull spilling out of their sockets
Flared nostrils at the long moment of your rupture

when screams do not match your mouth
You stagger into the circle of doubt
drawn by a stranger who knew you were coming

like a door opening before the knob is turned
Plants in a room swaying like seaweed
A woman swoons in the stands

as you go for your guts
holding on to what you can
You fall

The credit rolls
over the still of your hand
unfolding through lace cuffs

## Before America

White knuckles and greasy fingers back in Virginia.
It is the middle of an unusually green winter
as the landlord's maintenance man waits
in the laundryroom recalling sub-zero weather
in Oklahoma City and a truck
he never let go of—
I pull black socks clinging to white shirts,
think of snow falling as kids play touch football
between tenements; they shout down each other's "Mumma!"
My breath curls in the thin air
blowing out signals—Oklahoma
was never so near
staging its sunsets behind screen doors
for a woman ironing in her slip beneath a naked light bulb
I follow the drop of sweat falling down
her neck as the steam rises to her face
her husband churns up red dust in a tractor
using up the late daylight
and the telephone wires thread Virginia to Tennessee
to Arkansas—"Scottish Inn next five miles"—waves me
past the bandaid box silos in Texas and a blond boy
with a red cap spits on my car at a gas station
in Groon—
my car, my car—Detroit was that city
with the fake sunset and gray earth children
peeping through snow;
an old-timer told me about how a midwest soldier
lay for days
with one side of his face frozen to the ground.

It is Saturday Sweeping in Kansas
with an old broom counting the strokes
back and forth
chasing the dust back to the burning summer plains.
I hear the humming of rocks and a melting stream
between them filled with the carcasses of newly-thawed animals.
I get lost
in a raunchy bar in Denver and feel fingers
spelling out "I love you" yet as I turn
there is only smoke and the musicians
straining to be heard—
between the last breath of the fir trees and the air
are the stars as particles of blood
stream from the eyes of trucks heading for L.A.—
a place where one can have three names and no features.
As I turn again
to face the ocean the way I was told I would,
nothing comes; no one shouts
above the gilded silence

# Notes On A Recital

A white clock ticks on the wall
while a butter-colored moon drifts into place.

Two women enter in pastel kimonoes with black obes.
Carrying the koto they pause
to leave their red zoris beside the green carpet
like poppies grown out of the wooden floor.
*

The women place felt under the koto
to cushion sound. Nodding slowly
they tighten the strings, then reach
for false fingernails in the deep pockets
of their sleeves. One by one
each nail becomes an ivory pick.
*

They tune the koto
as a man in black kimono enters, offering
the shakuhachi. He bows to the women,
then kneels, gently turning its mouth
to his lips. He breathes

the cry of a sandpiper above waves. Sunflowers
rise like giants out of small gardens. Rice sprouting
on the paddy bank. Our sleeves swell
with those waves, the first song
of a mountain warbler above Kyoto. Autumn comes
to a blind master of koto arranging
and re-arranging his piece
                    *Shiki No Nagame,* in time
for the Emperor's birthday. Snow covers the mountain in Aug
while a white snake crawls out to eat morning dew.
We listen mutely while the moon
and pathways behind the wall
vanish in high grass.

## Every Scene We Walk Into Is Open-Ended

Like a great tongue stuck out
At the world, half a sun sets
Over yellowing pastures and cattle scattered
Like ashes — they sleep on land
Without contour
Like unqualified love given in a vacant room

A woman speaks a promise to herself at a window
The voice is monotonous
As she raises, then lowers the shade

## Birds In The Hand

The character of this moment
is a young Japanese-American
seated in a bus station, his head down
his fingers rubbing the bird
he has just made out of newspaper. The last letter
of the headline is on the tip of the left wing

He learned the art of origami at 5
when the time was right to know
that a perfect bird, dog, or butterfly
was a matter of tissue ... pale blue, yellow, green.

"It is more supple," his mother had told him.
She could make a dog in 2 minutes
and the foreigners would be amazed, try
their own versions and learn
that their hands were like thick dough
through which no beak, wing, or head could grow.

At the end of each creation
his mother would blow air into the body
then rise from her knees, slide open
the rice paper door and let in
the flat, white moon.

# IV.

# Voice in the Bowl

# Traveling Music

Turn into another driveway every other day.
A face that welcomes. Another to wave you on.
Always the beer to wash away the road.
Your friend shakes her head, not believing
you're here. Five years, she keeps repeating
and picks up where she left you. No accounting
for the stuff between. You are the unfinished house
in her jigsaw puzzle.

You catch up way past the baby's bedtime. Guilty,
you keep talking, knowing your hosts must get up at 6.
But you've come all this way, you think, let them listen.
They show you where to park your bag, where the john is.
They pat your shoulder goodnight and leave you listening
to the toilet flush. Their muffled sexless voices,
the clink of change on a dresser, the yawns
and midnight music on the digital clock
that shuts off by itself.

You feel the car spitting out white lines,
the fast lane and the woman from Missouri you passed.
Her sunglasses propped on her head, a two-year old
in a carseat. He is eating crackers
falling asleep as he chews. She pulls down the sun
visor, wipes the sweat from his forehead. Yes,
the sun was a fadeless argument that day.
Caught in the glare and the downtown sounds, she
disappears, another bead on the traffic string
through Cleveland. Your eyes fall into
the chair's striped upholstery and you swear
to drive at night tomorrow, keep vigil
with the truckers, cross state lines
on a thermos of coffee and a wonder drug.
Let the country singer kill you
drifting onto the shoulder to climb another tree.

## Rilke's Daydream

the cleaning woman is late
he puts on her apron to polish his piano
        he feels it set in
like a gash in the smooth wood
his zealous cloth purring as it intersects the grain

he dreams he is a street sweeper
    who dreams his is a reaper
        swinging his broom across an asphalt field
          across the lacquered surface
              he would make a mirror with a scythe

in field, alcove and attic
in her apron he is housed everywhere
        but nowhere shut in

she enters the foyer laughing
        Mein Herr!
      he does not hear     being both
        figure
and ground

## White Cat In The Shell, Moon On The Wane

I live in the country of unanswered letters,
in a basement where snow falls in the stairwell.
            There is no exit
while the moon loses the full shape of its creamy face.
A truck is hauling a coffin to a barren field.
The man inside is accused of solitude
and made to answer for his stolen time.
A dawn runner is chased by yelping dogs,
purple clouds bruising the sky.

A white cat occupies a faded green sofa left on the roadside —
            someone wanting to change
            the looks of a favorite room
            or someone with no room left

The cat adheres to the old sofa
like a turtle to its carapace, like Quasimodo
to his cathedral, the snail taking the form of its shell.
It is his home, his hole
            his envelope.

## Dwarf In The Rock

The sun is no ally when you're chiseling away at the stone
in your driveway. You look grimly at the Michelangelo clouds
racing across the sky. A dwarf inside the granite is scratching
his way out. He is unsure of himself and asks you stupid
questions: How tall am I? How much do I weigh? Am I a blom
What am I wearing? Am I supposed to smile? Am I even
representational? Whose idea was this anyway?

There is a tapping that will not go away
and his whispers become a roar
as the sun bears down harder
on your naked back and the beer is gone.
Your dripping eyelids close as you collapse
beside the stone, curling up inside its shade.
You wait for the kidnapping.
Whatever is inside
has better places to go than you.

# Sleepwalking

Mother had an unfurnished room
where she would go every day and dance to Strauss waltzes
alone, in a pale blue gown.
She would trace his face on the window pane—
the man in Minnesota who promised to return
in the autumn of any year.

*Sleepwalking on a frozen lake, the young girl removes*
*her gingham dress as a last gesture to the cold.*
*She has been lured to a moment*
*that sings out to her like an aria.*

Once Father heard us laughing in the middle of a board meeting,
came home to take Mother in his arms.
They danced in the kitchen. She whispered in his ear,
"I was hoping you would come." He smiled, pretending to believe
her flattery—"Baby, let me teach you the Linoleum Foxtrot."

*The man from Minnesota wears a blue tie,*
*white swan on a blue field*
*cloud in the lake*
*cloud becoming swan*
*swimming out of the lake*
*swan drowning*
*swan threaded into blue cloth*
*the man from Minnesota wears a lake around his neck*
*he is diving in to save the swan*
*he is drowning*

*the swan is wearing his blue tie*
*his face is threaded into the tie*
*he is smiling*
*the swan beats her wings on his desk*
*Mother's letters fly like feathers out the window*

If we give objects the friendship they deserve
we do not open a wardrobe without a slight start.
Beneath its russet wood, a wardrobe is a very white almond.
To open it when sleepwalking
is to experience an event of whiteness. The center of the lock
is sculpted in the form of a lizard, crocodile, or turtle
or two human figures: the first man, the first woman.

## The Doodler

He draws circles on a plastic tablecloth.
With a felt tip pen he goes round and round.
His wife asks, "Coming to bed?"
He answers, "Later. I'm working."

He is in the middle of some risk, this
continuous circling, this blueprint for a cave.
He decides they have lived too long above ground.

He remembers first year French in the ninth grade,
the pictures of those great cave murals in southern France
just before the chapter on the conditional tense —

a great bull frozen in his fear,
a spear thrust deep into his neck.
The hunter is a stick figure in the background.
This could be, he thinks, the first cartoon.

He rests his head on the tablecloth,
leans against the dying bull on the wall.

Filling in the spaces between the flowers,
he thinks, "I'll hang it on the wall before she gets up —
Studies in Dots and Daisies." He laughs.
He goes round and round.

## Banks Close Too Early For Painters

Take only what is needed.
Turning painters over in their graves
We find chalk in their eyes, the possibility

Of "Fish Magic" cannot be
Taken for granted. If only
Perfect shapes were never thought of.

If only I could rememeber the last digit
Of that number to keep the check from going through.
Banks close too early for painters

Whose days begin at dusk
When dollar bills flutter down gratefully
Onto acrylic, say spend me thoroughly

On this blessed surface. It is all
We need to know from each object that consents
To be a part of "Guernica." The silence

Rubs in, takes hold. The unworthiness of certain cloths
Spread-eagles itself when the lights are dim
And proletarian martyrs pick the rubies from their pockets—

"Out! Out! We cannot live this way any longer!
We must be what they said we were!"

Off they go to hide in the cellars of definition
Scraping off the tiles with their long nails
And hard teeth. They vomit some design

Into the present. Sleep well, painters.
We won't ask you to tell us your dreams.

# Intersection At The Zero Hour

You wait for the end of winter.
An Ethiopian soldier waits for moonrise
pacing the narrow beach along the Red Sea.
He sees each wave, a slash against the sand;
every crab alert to the sound of his sentry.

You wait for the snow to melt;
The soldier waits for the light
to go out in the general's tent.
A naked bulb sways above a wave of cobweb.
Snow flies over the highway, white hair
pulled from the head of a madwoman.
The soldier feels the pulse of his rifle
against his heaving chest.

You know the limits, towns
you have driven through
in the hours before dawn; you have lived
in cold houses warmed by your dreams. The soldier
smiles, his rifle raised to the ghostly tent.

You are lost in a distant corridor
filling slowly with the Red Sea;
the general's heart frozen
by the grace of perfect timing.
The soldier walks through your town.
You whisper, "Stay," and hear the snow
in his ear, melting, wave.

## Voice In The Bowl

You sink deeper into impossible avenues,
sequestered by waves, holding fast to the desert.
Rabbits scurry across the road where you run.
No greeting, just flight.
The green hills roll joyfully on to the Mississippi
while combines spit out black dirt.
A farmer's CB keeps him company at dusk
in his beanfield, he loses all connections.
What next? What next?
It is the only question in the thicket of wonder.

Trapped cottontail tries to get his attention.
Your typewriter rattles on into the dawn,
fingers gone numb. They yield to the sun for power . . .
give it back. *Give it back.* Comes a voice so small,
girlchild in a red snowsuit, blond curls leaking out.
She runs into the chicken coop behind her grandfather.
The hens scatter at the sight of red,
lose their eggs. *Little girl, little girl,*
*you are bad for business.* Grandpa's nine fingers
gather what they can before the sun's too high.
Rhode Island Reds scuttle around his tractor,
lose themselves in the feed.

The day curls into a hayroll. Girl, grandpa, and chickens
careen in the bowl of wonder.
What next? What next?

# The Planet Is Too Cold For The Invaders

Loose gray hairs on the librarian's sweater
remind her to watch the sleeping boy
wake up to his anatomy text, her youth

in the backseat of a borrowed car.
He has but one leg and kills time
in the pinball arcade, waiting for a ride
to his one room apartment.

He ponders the convenience of living in Biology.
Could set up housekeeping in the janitor's closet.
Nothing fancy, just functional.

Buckets could be turned over for seats.
He could stare forever
at the upflung hair of brooms leaning in the corner.

The librarian snaps the binder shut
on the most recent government document.
The one-legged boy can't keep his eyes off

the sci-fi novel in his lap. He hears the librarian
say, "I have been waiting for you almost a century."

Her hair falls across her eyes
and he feels the ship careening toward Earth,
great blue-green crescent in its first quarter.

## Waiting For Instruction

In a closed room a porcelain Buddha stares
Into Venetian blinds
Zebra stripes on the wall
On my sister exercising
In a white leotard

The record skips
Yet she does not notice
The refrain      I remember how she wore
Mother's dresses      Wide gestures
To an invisible audience
Tripping on the long hem
And the high heels she could only fill
Half way
Her cornstalk curls spilling from a pillbox hat
Black netting over her small face
Caged childwoman

Now she lifts her leg
Onto the highest rung of a straightback chair
Bending until her face touches her knee
She holds the position
As if waiting for instruction

A breeze rattles the Venetian blinds
Passing through the room briefly
It swirls in the tiny eyes of the Buddha